Try This At Home!

Impressive Dance Moves

Ellen Labrecque

Raintree is an imprint of Capstone Global Library Limited, a company incorporated in England and Wales having its registered office at 7 Pilgrim Street, London, EC4V 6LB – Registered company number: 6695582

To contact Raintree please phone 0845 6044371, fax + 44 (0) 1865 312263, or email myorders@ raintreepublishers.co.uk. Customers from outside the UK please telephone +44 1865 312262.

Text © Capstone Global Library Limited 2013
First published in hardback in 2013
Paperback edition first published in 2014
The moral rights of the proprietor have been asserted.

Edited by Rebecca Rissman, Daniel Nunn, and Adrian Vigliano
Designed by Cynthia Della-Rovere
Picture research by Elizabeth Alexander
Production by Alison Parsons
Originated by Capstone Global Library Ltd
Printed and bound in China by China Translation and Printing Services Ltd

ISBN 978 1 406 25102 9 (hardback)
16 15 14 13 12
10 9 8 7 6 5 4 3 2 1

ISBN 978 1 406 25109 8 (paperback)
17 16 15 14 13
10 9 8 7 6 5 4 3 2 1

British Library Cataloguing in Publication Data
Labrecque, Ellen.
Impressive dance moves. -- (Try this at home!)
792.8-dc23
A full catalogue record for this book is available from the British Library.

Acknowledgements
We would like to thank the following for permission to reproduce photographs: © Capstone Publishers pp. 8 t, 8 b, 9 t, 9 b, 10, 11, 12, 13 t, 13 b, 14 t, 14 b, 15 t, 15 b, 16 t, 16 b, 17, 18, 19 t, 19 b, 20, 21 t, 21 b, 22, 23 t, 23 b, 24 t, 24 b, 25 t, 25 b, 26, 27 t, 27 b (Karon Dubke); Getty images pp. 4 (Granger Wootz/Blend Images), 28 (Image Source), 29 (altrendo images/Stockbyte); SuperStock pp. 5 (© fStop), 6 (© Richard B. Levine/Ambient Images Inc.), 7 (© Image Source). Design features reproduced with the permission of Shutterstock (© CAN BALCIOGLU), (© Nadezda), (© Merve Poray), (© Nicemonkey).

Cover photograph of a modern style dancer reproduced with permission of Shutterstock (© Ayakovlev).

Every effort has been made to contact copyright holders of material reproduced in this book. Any omissions will be rectified in subsequent printings if notice is given to the publisher.

All the internet addresses (URLs) given in this book were valid at the time of going to press. However, due to the dynamic nature of the internet, some addresses may have changed, or sites may have changed or ceased to exist since publication. While the author and publisher regret any inconvenience this may cause readers, no responsibility for any such changes can be accepted by either the author or the publisher.

Contents

Some words are shown in bold, **like this**. You can find out what they mean by looking in the Glossary.

Let's dance!

Everybody and anybody can dance. The trick is to look good while doing it. How do you do that? By learning the coolest moves around!

Your friends will want to groove just like you after you master the moves in this book. All you need to do is practise. Let's get ready to boogie, rock, shimmy, and dance the night and day away!

Be safe

You don't need a helmet or safety pads for dancing. But you should wear comfortable clothing and shoes, so that you can move around easily without tripping or falling.

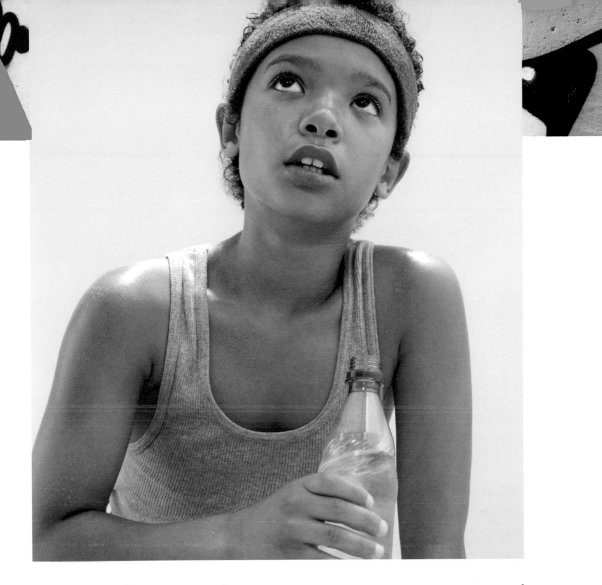

Dancing is exercise – you may even work up a sweat. If you want to dance, it is important to stay fit. Don't forget to take rest breaks and drink plenty of water to stay **hydrated**. Then, you can get back on the dance floor and get going. Let's learn some moves!

The spin

Level of difficulty:
Easy

STEP 1

The spin is simple. First, bend your knees slightly and put your hands out to your side to help you stay balanced.

STEP 2

To spin to your left, plant your left foot behind your right and turn your upper body to the right to gain **momentum**.

STEP 3

Lift your right foot and bring it around your body as you keep your left toes planted.

Spin to the **beat** of the song.

STEP 4

Spin your body all the way around to face the same direction. Step out with your right foot to stop spinning.

9

Moonwalk

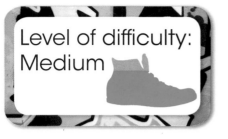
The moonwalk was made popular by **legendary** pop star Michael Jackson.

STEP 1

To begin, lift your left leg so that only your toes are on the floor.

STEP 2

Place your right foot about 30 centimetres (12 inches) in front of your left. Slide your right heel back so it is even with your left.

Snap the left heel down and raise the right heel at the same time, so that now the right toes are touching the floor.

Repeat this move again and again. The smoother you glide, the cooler it looks!

The robot

STEP **1**

When you do the robot, you want to look **rigid**. Bend your arms at the elbow in a 90-degree angle. Slowly raise them, one at a time, so that your open palms reach eye level.

Slowly turn your head from right to left, again and again.

STEP

Now try walking. As you raise one arm, take a step, keeping your legs bent slightly at the knees.

STEP

While keeping your back **taut**, stiffly bend at the waist once in a while to add flair to the dance.

Criss-cross

STEP 1

Stand with your legs shoulder-width apart and your knees bent.

STEP 2

Jump straight up in the air and, as you hop up, criss-cross your legs.

STEP 3

Jump up again and criss-cross your legs the other way.

STEP 4

Land with your legs shoulder-width apart, and then rock side to side four times.

Repeat the first two steps again and face a new direction each time. This dance looks great with a big group!

15

The worm

STEP 1

Lie face down on the floor and put your arms on the ground in a push-up position. Your stomach should still be on the floor.

STEP 2

Kick your legs up. Right before your legs reach the ground again, do a push-up.

STEP **3**

When your toes touch the ground again, kick out and do another push-up. Inch up a little bit on every move.

Make your body as loose as possible and keep repeating these steps. You want a wave-like motion to run through your body.

The arm wave

STEP 1

With this move, you want your body to look **fluid**. Hold both arms straight out to your side.

Begin with your right hand. Curl your hand down and raise your elbow at the same time. Lift your shoulder and straighten out your arm on an angle.

18

STEP 2

Continue the movement to the other (left) shoulder. Lift your left shoulder, then put it down and lift up your elbow.

STEP 3

Straighten out your arm and point your wrist downwards. Then bring the move back to the other side.

The clown

STEP 1

The clown uses the arm wave as part of the move. Begin by shaking both hands from the wrist like you are trying to shake water off of them.

STEP 2

As you shake your hands, bend your knees and pop up and down.

STEP 3

Go up and down four times, then switch to the arm wave.

Do the arm wave twice, then go back to the first movement. Make sure your body is loose and flowing from move to move.

The Tut

STEP 1

The Tut is all about stiff-arm poses. It is most important to keep your hands flat and fingers together. Hold one arm in front of you and bend it at the elbow at a right angle. Then bend your flat palm down at another right angle.

STEP 2

Bend your other arm the opposite way. Your forearm is pointing down, and your flat palm is pointing behind you.

STEP 3

Take small, stiff steps forwards.

23

Everyday moves

STEP 1

You can **imitate** real-life stuff and do it on the dance floor! Spin around like a sprinkler.

STEP 2

Pretend to go shopping. Push the trolley along and reach up high for "food" on the shelves. Put it into your trolley.

Pretend to sprinkle your food with salt and pepper. Hold a shaker in each hand.

Pretend to bake a cake. Stir all the ingredients together. Put your whole body into the stirring motion.

Melting

Melting is a way
to move from one
dance move to
another. Move
slowly when you
melt. To practise,
start by standing
straight with your
arms up in the air.

26

STEP 2

Next, start to lean back and bend your knees to bring your whole body down slowly.

STEP 3

It is like your muscles are relaxing and your body is "melting". The slower you go, the more slick the **transition**.

How to look smooth

You want to look **fluid** on the dance floor. Here are five tips for how to look your best.

1. Listen to the music. The more aware you are of the **tempo** and **beat**, the better you'll do.

2. The best dancers are the ones who dance like nobody is watching.

3. Dance to your favourite music. If you like what you hear, you'll enjoy dancing more.

4. Practise in front of a mirror.

5. Have fun. The more fun you have, the better you'll dance!

Glossary

beat sound made by a steady rhythm; like the beat of a drum

fluid move or make a change easily and with grace

hydrate supply water to a person in order for them to remain healthy

imitate mimic or do the same thing as another person

legendary famous or celebrated

momentum keeping your body in motion

rigid stiff or difficult to bend

taut tightly stretched or tense

tempo speed at which a piece of music is played

transition movement of your body from one position to another

Find out more

Books

Dance, Andre Grau (Dorling Kindersley, 2005)

Dance Culture: Street Dance (Radar), Liz Gogerly
 (Wayland, 2011)

Street Dance (Master This), Emma Torrington
 (Wayland, 2010)

Websites

www.activitytv.com/dance-for-kids
Learn some more dance moves that are easy to do.

www.dancemagazine.com
A place to find out what's happening in the world
of dance.

www.danceuk.org
The national site for dance in the United Kingdom.

Index